Greek terracotta figures

1,00

1

R. A. Higgins

GREEK
TERRACOTTA
FIGURES

Published by The Trustees of The British Museum
LONDON 1963

Printed by Eyre and Spottiswoode Limited, Her Majesty's Printers, at the Grosvenor Press, Portsmouth

✻ *Contents*

Introduction   *page* 7

I The purpose of terracottas   9

II Technical processes   10

III The prehistoric period   12

IV The seventh and sixth centuries B.C.   14

V The fifth and fourth centuries B.C.   17

VI The Hellenistic period   23

Glossary   28

Bibliography   29

List of Plates   30

✢ Introduction

The chief use of fired clay – or terracotta – in antiquity was for domestic pottery. At a very early time, however, we may imagine a potter taking a spare piece of clay, making a model of one of his gods, his friends, or his animals, and firing it with his pots. For many centuries terracotta figures were no more than a by-product of the potter's craft, but eventually their manufacture achieved the status of a craft in its own right.

This booklet attempts to trace the history of Greek terracotta figures – commonly known as terracottas – with illustrations taken from the British Museum collections. Although the term terracotta is generally used to include large statues, architectural ornament, and decorative reliefs of this material, it is here restricted to statuettes, which form a distinct class, and are best considered alone.

❧ The purpose of terracottas

Terracottas were made in Greek lands from the Neolithic period down to the Roman Empire – a span of some 4,000 years – but they were by no means common before the second half of this long period. In Classical times we know that they were held in very low esteem beside major works of art, and this was probably their position at all times; but they are well worth our study today.

Terracottas were used in antiquity for several purposes. We learn from literary sources that many were made to serve as dolls and toys. Surviving examples are indeed frequently in this form, and Athenian tomb-monuments often depict women holding the toys of their childhood, which look very like surviving examples of terracotta. We learn also that statuettes were commonly dedicated in rustic shrines. The evidence of excavation gives a more complete picture; it reveals that terracottas were kept in private houses, were dedicated in shrines and temples, and were buried with the dead. As the subjects are at all periods predominantly religious, we may suppose that when found in houses they had frequently belonged to domestic shrines. Their function as votive offerings needs little comment, since most surviving examples are eminently suitable for this purpose. They were dedicated in temples and sanctuaries; when these places became too full, they were taken out and ceremoniously buried in trenches nearby, being frequently broken before burial to avoid being salvaged and re-used. As for those found in tombs, it would probably in general be correct to say that they were buried not for any specifically religious purpose, but as being the treasured possessions of the dead, like his (or her) pottery, jewellery, or weapons.

Most terracottas were equally suitable for domestic, votive, or funerary use, but certain exceptional varieties seem to have been specially designed for one purpose only. Some were made at temple-workshops for offering on the spot; and certain other types seem to have had an exclusively funerary purpose, such as the mourner on pl. 2.

Yet another use of terracotta statuettes may be noted in passing; they occasionally served as scent-bottles. Objects of this kind have in general been disregarded in this survey as being by nature vases rather than statuettes. One class has, however, been included as a vital stage in the evolution of the Greek terracotta. (See pl. 4.)

The clay, which is the basis of the terracotta, was (and is) so abundant in Greece that almost every community had its own clay-beds and made its own terracottas – a fact of great importance for the archaeologist, since the origin of a terracotta can frequently be determined by the clay of which it is made. The natural clay is refined and mixed with some other substance, such as sand, to reduce shrinkage during the drying and firing.

There are several ways in which statuettes could be fashioned. Hand-modelling is the simplest, was for a long time the only method, and needs no further comment. Another way is to make a hollow figure such as a cone or a cylinder on the potter's wheel, and to adapt it by hand to human or animal shape.

By far the most effective method, and the commonest from about 500 B.C. onwards, is moulding. The first requirement for this process is an original model, of wax or fired clay, from which a clay mould is taken. As a general rule a mould was needed only for the front, but occasionally the back was also moulded. The mould is touched up by hand, if necessary, and fired; it is then ready for use.

To make a statuette, wet clay is pressed into the mould. If a solid figure is wanted, the mould is completely filled with clay; but if, as was more usual in antiquity, a hollow figure is envisaged, the clay forms only a thin layer. When it has dried and is 'leather-hard', the clay impression is removed from the mould. The figure is built up from a number of separately made parts, stuck together with liquid clay. For a simple piece, all that is required is to attach the front and the back, which latter may be moulded like the front, or may be a piece of clay roughly shaped to fit.

A more ambitious piece is assembled from any number of separate parts. In a hollow piece, to avoid the risk of a 'blow-out' in the firing, the bottom is usually left open and in addition a vent is cut in the back.

These three methods of making terracottas could be used in combination, and were so used. For example, in the seventh and sixth centuries B.C. hand-made and wheel-made bodies were often equipped with moulded heads, and Hellenistic moulded figures frequently have hand-made additions.

When all was ready, the figures were fired in a potter's kiln, to a temperature ranging between 750 and 950 degrees Centigrade. Generally, ancient terracottas are rather softer than the contemporary vases, a sign that they were not fired at such a high temperature.

Terracottas were regularly decorated. Two distinct methods were employed. The first is the so-called glaze used on Greek vases from the Mycenaean period onwards. Applied before firing, it fired a shiny black or reddish-brown; the basic colour was sometimes supplemented by touches of white and purplish-red and by incised lines. This system was current in terracottas from the Early Bronze Age down to about 500 B.C.

The second process, by which matt colours were laid over a white slip, first appeared in the seventh century B.C., and became general by the end of the sixth. The figure was covered, before firing, with a slip of white clay; after firing, tempera colours were laid over the slip. A wide range of colours was employed, black, red, yellow, blue and green being regularly found. Unfortunately, these colours, originally much gayer than the glaze decoration, do not survive well, and in many cases have completely disappeared. Consequently, while we can often see a glaze-painted terracotta in its original condition, it is more difficult to visualize the original appearance of the matt-painted variety.

Terracottas of the Late Neolithic period and the Early Bronze Age in Greece, about 3,000–2,000 B.C., are hand-made and mostly very crude. An honourable exception is the recently-discovered 'Aphrodite of Lerna' in Argos Museum, an astonishingly mature work for such an early period (about 3,000 B.C.).[†] In Crete, in the Middle Minoan period (2000–1550 B.C.) figures of men, women, and animals were dedicated in sanctuaries, and were occasionally buried with the dead. The British Museum possesses a few such offerings, mostly fragmentary, from a sanctuary at Petsofa in East Crete.

It is not till the later part of the Mycenaean period (1400–1100 B.C.) that we can speak of anything like a terracotta industry. Mycenaean terracottas are extremely numerous on sites throughout the Aegean and beyond, wherever Mycenaeans settled, and they are remarkably similar wherever found, from South Italy to Syria. Surprisingly, very few have been found in Crete, where figures of an entirely different kind were popular. Like their counterparts of the Classical period, Mycenaean terracottas have been found in houses, in votive deposits and in tombs. Standing female figures, believed to be goddesses, are the most popular subjects. The modelling is stylized in the extreme, details such as the features and the drapery being added in reddish glaze. The goddesses wear long dresses, reaching to the ground, and (frequently) crown-like spreading head-dresses. The commonest varieties are shown on pl. 1; they are known to archaeologists by the letters of the Greek alphabet which each happens somewhat to resemble.

The *phi* (Φ) type (pl. 1a) is the oldest. It evolved rather before 1400 B.C. and lasted until shortly after 1300. The goddess stands with her arms across her body; sometimes they are modelled or painted, sometimes (as here) they must be imagined. A variant has a baby at the breast. The *tau* (T) type (pl. 1b) has the arms folded rigidly across the breast. It was current from 1400–1200 B.C. in the form illustrated, and from 1200–1100 in a degenerate form. The *psi* (Ψ) type (pl. 1c) differs from the *phi* type in having the arms raised, perhaps in a gesture of benediction. It lasted from about 1300 to 1200 B.C. as here illustrated, and in a degenerate form for a further century.

[†] *See Illustrated London News for 12th Jan. 1957, p. 69.*

Other Mycenaean varieties are known, of which oxen and chariot-groups are represented in the British Museum, while enthroned goddesses, empty thrones, ploughing groups, and other animals can be seen in other collections.

The style of these terracottas is unimaginative in the extreme when compared with the brilliance of contemporary frescoes, ivories and engraved gems. This craft was, however, one of mass-production, and such simple figures were doubtless sold at very low prices.

The Mycenaean world came to an end about 1100 B.C. after a century of turmoil. It was probably now that the Dorians invaded Greece, bringing in their wake poverty and chaos, from which it took the country some four centuries to recover. The period between 1100 and 700 may be considered as one; it covers the Submycenaean, Protogeometric and Geometric pottery-styles.

The three centuries from 1100 to 800 B.C. were too impoverished for luxuries such as terracottas to be at all common. In fact, the total of surviving materal amounts to little more than a few dolls. In the eighth century Greece grew more prosperous, and the output of terracottas increased. Crude hand-made figures of men and animals predominated in tombs and sanctuaries. There were also a few wheel-made animals of a rather higher standard; a horse with a load of wine-jars represents this class in the British Museum.

The seventh century sees the real beginning of the Greek terracotta industry. About 700 B.C., influences from North Syria, Phoenicia and Cyprus, which had started as a trickle about 800 B.C., now came flooding in. This century covers the so-called Orientalizing period of Greek art, when the culture of the more civilized East was being re-discovered and assimilated. In terracottas a new technique and a new style made a simultaneous appearance.

The new technique is the use of the mould. At first only solid-moulding was employed, for relief-plaques and for heads attached to hand-made or wheel-made bodies. This innovation meant that an un-skilled worker could mass-produce terracottas of a much higher standard than before.

The new style, which came with the use of the mould, is today called rather fancifully the Dedalic style, after Daedalus, the legendary Cretan artist. The attribution is not entirely inappropriate, since the style does seem to have developed in Crete and to have spread from there to the rest of Greece. It is characterized by a particular way of representing the human head, a fashion ultimately of Egyptian origin, which reached the Greek world at second hand from the Oriental sources mentioned above. Not only terracottas, but also bronzes and stone sculptures were made in this, the first sculptural style since the Mycenaean period. The face is flat, with the hair arranged in a fringe over the forehead and falling down on either side of the face like a modern judge's wig. This sophisticated treatment is completely different from the primitive heads on eighth-century figures. The style changes somewhat during the seventh century, the heads becoming less angular and more lifelike.

A characteristic of this period, and of the following two centuries, is the prevalence of local styles. Every major community evolved its own peculiarities, in marked contrast to the astonishing uniformity of My-cenaean art. The chief centres of production in the seventh century were Rhodes, Crete, Corinth and Sparta. There are examples in the British Museum from all these centres.

Pl. 2 shows a typical Dedalic terracotta from Rhodes of about 670 B.C., with a hand-made body and a moulded head. It was evidently made specially for funerary use, since it depicts a female mourner. Originally she was tearing her hair with both hands in the traditional gesture of mourning; her right arm is now missing. Red-filled scratches on breast and cheeks indicate where she has already drawn blood.

A more complicated seventh-century piece is shown on colour pl. A. Two women are seated side by side. As in the previous pieces, the heads are moulded and the bodies hand-made, but instead of being cylindrical they are flat. The faces are in the developed Dedalic style of about 625 B.C. Although this piece is believed to have been found at Thebes, the clay and the style indicate that it was made in Corinth. The details are indicated in glaze. The women are probably the earth-goddesses Demeter and Persephone, who, although mother and daughter, were sometimes represented identically at this period. They sit on the seat of a country-cart. It was originally equipped with a pole and a body, presumably of wood, and was probably drawn by terracotta beasts. The goddesses wear the peplos and the divine headdress, the polos.

In the sixth century the principal areas of production were an unidentified East Greek centre, Corinth, Argos, Attica and Boeotia. All these areas are represented in the British Museum, Boeotia particularly well. Terracottas followed much the same course as in the seventh century, except for one class, which will be considered shortly. On pl. 3 is a typical Boeotian terracotta, of about 570–550 B.C. The body is still as flat as before, with no attempt at modelling apart from rudimentary arms; but the moulded head follows the increase in naturalism which is to be seen in contemporary sculpture. The details are indicated in a good black glaze, picked out with red. Her high polos suggests that she is a goddess; to judge from the pomegranate-ornament on her necklace, she should be Demeter or Persephone.

Boeotia was particularly rich in terracottas from the sixth century onwards. A popular variety existed side by side with that illustrated on pl. 3; it had a similar body but a crude hand-made head with virtually no indication of the features. Another common type consists of a horse and rider, the horse striped like a zebra and the rider without legs. Both these varieties are represented in the British Museum.

Somewhere in the Eastern Greek world, perhaps in Rhodes or perhaps in Samos, the picture was different. Shortly before 600 B.C. potters started to make, with the aid of moulds, scent-bottles in human and animal form; they decorated them in the usual way, with black glaze, helped out with added red and white and with incision. These scent-bottles soon became extremely popular and were exported throughout the Greek world and beyond, especially into Etruria. It would seem that they were treasured as much for themselves as for the scent which they contained. Favourite subjects are gorgon's heads (after which the class has been christened the Gorgoneion class), female busts, warrior's heads, animal-heads and complete animals. This class is well represented in the British Museum amongst the finds from the cemeteries of Camirus in Rhodes.

About 550 B.C. a new type of scent-bottle evolved. The style was modernized to conform with the advances made in sculpture; the size was increased, complete human figures being introduced; and a new method of decoration was adopted. In place of the black pottery-glaze, brilliant matt colours were laid over a white slip (see p. 11). When new, these figures must have looked much more brilliant than the 'Gorgoneion' class, which is no doubt why the new kind so quickly ousted the old.

Another innovation is associated with this class. In certain examples the spout is entirely omitted, so that the figure is not a scent-bottle but a statuette. Such statuettes are the source from which stemmed all the hollow-moulded terracottas with which the subsequent chapters will be concerned. Both kinds, the scent-bottle and the statuette, are illustrated on pl. 4. Both were made about 540–530 B.C., and were found at Camirus in Rhodes. That on the right is a scent-bottle, that on the left a statuette, but they are otherwise almost identical. They represent the goddess Aphrodite, wearing a chiton and mantle and holding one of her attributes, a dove. Her sleek, well-fed appearance is typical of East Greek art of this period. The backs of these pieces are as well modelled as the fronts and the moulded surfaces have been carefully retouched. Altogether, so well designed and well made are they that they have every right to be considered as minor works of sculpture. The repertoire of this class includes seated women, squatting satyrs, sirens (woman-headed birds), and animals. All these varieties are represented in the British Museum, principally from the cemeteries of Camirus.

A *Corinthian goddesses, about* 620 B.C.

B *Aphrodite and Eros, about* 350 B.C.

By 500 B.C. moulded figures, sometimes solid but more usually hollow, were common but were not yet universal. The type illustrated on pl. 5 was made in Athens from about 510 to about 470 B.C. It occurs in many sizes. These figures were made solid, the front moulded and the back flat, and the larger ones were afterwards partly hollowed out underneath. The decoration is in matt paint. A goddess sits stiffly on a throne, her feet on a footstool and her hands resting on her lap. There is practically no modelling on her body but the drapery is indicated in paint, in some examples very elaborately. She wears a chiton, a mantle which goes over her head, and in her curly hair a large diadem. Her jewellery consists of earrings and, in many examples, several necklaces.

We may suppose that the goddess represented is Athena. In some examples her aegis is actually painted on the breast. To judge from the clay, the majority, if not all, of the surviving examples were made in Athens; many have indeed been found there, for the most part buried in trenches on the Acropolis after the Persian sack of 480 B.C. It is possible that these figures are copied from the venerable wooden cult-statue of Athena Polias which was kept in the Erechtheum, but the evidence is not conclusive.

Another type, also found on the Acropolis, consists of a young woman standing, wearing a chiton and transverse mantle. This type, not present in the British Museum, possibly represents a worshipper of Athena rather than the goddess herself.

In the early fifth century a special class of terracotta was very popular in Boeotia, and was copied elsewhere. These pieces were hand-made, but were very carefully modelled, thanks no doubt to the influence of the mould. People are represented in the course of their everyday occupations; a woman makes bread, puts a loaf in the oven, teaches her child to cook; a barber cuts a customer's hair; a carpenter saws a piece of wood. The British Museum is not rich in this class, but it has numbers of animals, some with riders, which we may regard as offshoots of it. One of these terracottas, which were probably intended as toys, is shown on pl. 6a. A bearded man, wearing an Oriental headdress, rides on a goose. The colours are unusually well preserved: the rider's headdress is red and his garment blue; his flesh is pink and his beard and moustache black. Other pieces of this class include a boy on a horse, a boy on a dolphin, a dog, a goat, a ram and a deer.

Good hand-made toys were also popular in Corinth; here they were made right down to about 330 B.C. Satyrs, monkeys, mules and other creatures are portrayed in an amusing manner. Pl. 6b shows a monkey sitting at a mortar, holding a pestle in its left hand and putting a cake into its mouth with the right. This piece was made in Corinth about 420 B.C.

But these pieces are exceptional. The typical figure of the fifth century is hollow-moulded, a process derived from the East Greek scent-bottles and related figures of the later sixth century. They are more plentiful than their predecessors, but technically inferior, being carelessly mass-produced; and stylistically they tend to lag behind the spirit of the times. Backs are no longer moulded, and frequently have large, unsightly vents, and retouching is seldom employed. The principal centres were now Rhodes, Athens, Corinth, and Boeotia. Although Boeotia and the Italian and Sicilian Greeks still retained certain peculiarities, which will be discussed below, there is a feeling of uniformity throughout most of the Greek world, in marked contrast to the pronounced local styles of the seventh and sixth centuries.

In sculpture we rightly draw a distinction between the rich style of the Late Archaic period (500–475 B.C.) and the austerity of the Early Classical (475–440). This distinction has little validity as far as terracottas are concerned, where the early style simply shades off into the later. The maker of terracottas evidently obtained his ideas at second-hand, and any innovations had lost their intitial impact by the time they reached him. On pl. 7a is an Athenian figure of a woman of about 450 B.C., wearing a peplos. The vertical-horizontal emphasis is typical of the sculptures of the middle years of the fifth century, and is seen to perfection in the figures from the Temple of Zeus at Olympia. This style, which has been aptly named the Severe Style, soon fell out of favour in sculpture, but its influence on terracottas was considerably longer-lived.

In Boeotia, hand-made figures and groups ceased to be made about 470 B.C., but Boeotian terracottas continued to pursue a course of their own throughout the fifth century and beyond. They deserve a special mention not only for their highly individual style, but also for the great numbers in which they were produced. Two principle varieties may be noted. The first consists of standing female figures not unlike those made in the rest of Greece, but considerably larger, with larger vents in the back, and higher bases. In the middle of the fifth century the women wear tall headdresses of a peculiarly Boeotian form; towards the end of the century they wear a low polos surmounting a bulky and highly elaborate arrangement of the hair, an arrangement found nowhere else in the Greek world. Pl. 7b shows such a figure of about 430 B.C. It derives from such Severe Style figures as that illustrated on pl. 7a. The hand is raised to the breast in an archaic gesture which had survived into the later fifth century in the conservative craft of terracotta work-ing. The second variety consists of statuettes of youths, naked except for a cloak draped over the back and shoulders, and holding a cock in the crook of the left arm. Towards the end of the fifth century the elaborate hairdressing of the youths comes to resemble that of the con-temporary female figures. This type, well represented in the British Museum, was made in vast quantities and in a variety of sizes.

The fourth century sees a revival of standards in the design and crafts-manship of terracottas throughout the Greek world. Side by side with commonplace pieces, comparable with work of the preceding century, we see to an increasing extent terracottas of a higher quality, echoing (however faintly) the great works of sculpture of the fourth century.

Such a piece is illustrated on colour plate B. It was found at Olbia in South Russia, but is too good to have been made at this outpost of Greek culture. To judge from the clay, it may have been made at Corinth, but we cannot be sure. The date is about 350 B.C. Aphrodite and a childish Eros stand together on a semi-circular base. She is per-forming a stately dance, to which Eros beats time on a tambourine. Her softly voluptuous face echoes the style of Praxiteles. Apart from the charming composition and the careful workmanship, the range of colours is unusually wide: pale blue, dark blue, red, two shades of pink, yellow and black. Instead of the usual chalky surface, the white slip has a high gloss, which gives an enamel-like sheen to the colours laid over it.

In general, the increasing uniformity which was apparent in Greek terracottas in the fifth century is even more noticeable in the fourth. In Boeotia, however, side by side with echoes of sculptural types common to the rest of Greece, we find continuations of the characteristic local figures of the fifth century, with their high bases and their peculiar fashion of hairdressing.

In the fourth century, comic actors, wearing grotesque masks and the traditional padded costume, form a very popular subject. This preference, which seems to have originated in Athens, soon spread to the rest of Greece. In view of the religious nature of most Greek terracottas, such a choice of subject might cause surprise, but it should be remembered that dramatic performances, comic as well as tragic, were in origin religious ceremonies, and never completely lost this function.

These pieces were evidently made (and sold) in sets, each set comprising the complete cast of one play. There are two such sets in the Metropolitan Museum in New York, from a tomb in Athens. The plays which they represent belong to the so-called Middle Comedy of the mid-fourth century B.C.: later than the Old Comedy of Aristophanes but earlier than the New Comedy of Menander. Two examples are illustrated, both Athenian, of about 350 B.C., contemporary with the sets in New York mentioned above. On pl. 8a is an actor playing the part of a young woman; an actor rather than an actress, since all the parts were played by men. On pl. 8b is a stock comic character, a slave who has run away from his master and has taken sanctuary on an altar. He sardonically raises a hand to his ear, indicating that he is deaf to appeals to leave the safety of the altar.

It was noted above that dolls were one of the commonest forms of Greek terracottas. The earliest dolls are bell-shaped figures with movable legs, which were made from the tenth to the eighth century. There is then a gap in the series, which starts again about 500 B.C. The chief centres for the production of dolls in the fifth and fourth centuries were Corinth and Athens. In Corinthian dolls (well represented in the British Museum), the body is moulded solid; arms and legs were made separately and attached by cords or wires. The figures take the form of dancers, and many hold castanets or a tambourine; in the top of the head is a hole, evidently for a peg to which a cord was attached, so that the doll could be made to dance like a modern puppet. Some examples are clothed, whilst others are naked. The latter are probably intended to be dressed by their young owners. Pl. 8c shows a naked Corinthian doll of about 350 B.C., found in Corinth; it originally held castanets in both hands.

Athenian dolls are also well represented in the British Museum. They were made in several forms, the commonest being very like the Corinthian except that the body is hollow.

The Greek colonies of Sicily and South Italy have yet to be considered. They were producing terracottas in vast quantities from about 500 B.C. onwards in a number of distinctive styles. The most important local styles are those of Sicilian Greeks, and of the South Italian Greek colonies of Tarentum, Locri, and Paestum.

The Sicilian colonies produced several varieties which are well represented in the British Museum, mostly from Gela. One variety, illustrated on pl. 9, flourished from about 500 to 450 B.C. A goddess is seated on a wide throne, her feet on a footstool and her hands on her lap. She wears a tall polos, a peplos fastened at the shoulders with large brooches, and three rows of pectoral ornaments consisting of pendants threaded on cords or chains. These ornaments have been connected with certain gold plaques found in seventh century Rhodian tombs; but they have more in common with Argive terracottas of the sixth century. It is not known which goddess is represented.

Another variety, consisting of a standing woman holding a pig, must be connected with the worship of Demeter and Persephone, to whom the pig was sacred. It started about 500 and went on, changing with the current changes in style, till about 330 B.C.

The terracottas from Locri in many ways resemble those from Sicily, but are made of a different clay. The most characteristic products of Locrian workshops were not, however, statuettes but decorative reliefs, which are outside the scope of this booklet.

On pl. 10 is a representative of a type made at the Greek colony of Paestum (near Salerno) and found in large quantities near the temples at Paestum and at the mouth of the river Sele nearby. To judge from the dedications of the temples, the goddess represented is Hera, the consort of Zeus and Queen of the gods. She sits stiffly on a throne with an ornamental back and a footstool, wearning earrings, a chiton, a mantle draped symmetrically over her head and shoulders, and (over the top of the mantle) a polos. Her hands rest on her lap; in the right is a dish for pouring libations, and in the left a bowl of fruit. This piece was probably made about 400 B.C., although the stiffness of the pose recalls an earlier period. Another common Paestan type (of which there are examples in the British Museum) consists of a woman standing, holding a sacred casket on her left shoulder, and pressing a young pig to her breast with her right hand. Like her Sicilian counterpart, she must be connected with the worship of Demeter or Persephone.

The terracottas of Tarentum (the modern Taranto) have many peculiar features. They represent for the most part the god Dionysus reclining on a couch. In some examples a woman sits at his feet, frequently holding a naked male child. The woman is believed to be Persephone, the child Iacchus. These pieces are unusually flat, something between a statuette and a relief; many are supported behind by struts of clay like the supports of modern photograph-frames. Some 30,000 figures, mostly of this kind, were found in a votive deposit at Tarentum, and this is the source of the majority of the Tarentine terracottas in the British Museum.

The reclining Dionysus figures range in date from 500 to 330 B.C. Complete examples are rare, coming as they do from a votive deposit rather than from tombs (see p. 9), but an extremely fine fragment is illustrated on pl. 11. It shows a woman and child from the feet of a reclining Dionysus, of about 350 B.C. There is a monumental quality about it which recalls the sculptures of the great fourth-century masters.

The conquests of Alexander the Great between 333 and 322 B.C. changed the face of the Greek world. Two characteristics of the new age, known as the Hellenistic period, are particularly important to our subject. In the first place, the attitude to established religion became more sceptical, and gods tended to be represented in a less reverent way. Secondly, the processes started in the fifth century were finally completed: regional differences in art were almost completely obliterated, and we find a uniformity throughout the Greek world which had not been seen since Mycenaean days.

About the same time, for causes which are largely unknown to us, Greek terracottas reached a peak of technical perfection not seen since the sixth century, and for the next three and a half centuries they may be regarded as real, if minor, works of sculpture. Before this time, it had been customary to use either one mould, or at most two; henceforth, terracottas were made from any number of elements, made separately (in moulds or freehand) and attached before firing, such as heads, fronts, backs, bases, arms, and minor additions.

The Early Hellenistic period, 330–200 B.C., is characterized by the so-called Tanagra style. This style acquired its name in the seventies of last century when the first, and for long the finest, examples were found in the illicitly-excavated cemeteries of the Boeotian town of Tanagra. As a style it has great charm, but it has been spoilt for many people by forgeries which flooded the market when the supply of genuine 'Tanagras' ran out.

We now know that examples as fine as those from Tanagra were made in Athens, and that is doubtless where the style originated. Outside Athens and Tanagra, the best pieces come from Alexandria in Egypt, where immigrant Athenian craftsmen may well have worked. The style was copied, often in a rather debased form, throughout the Hellenistic world.

The commonest subject is a woman standing in a statuesque but entirely natural pose. The backs are frequently moulded, though seldom with as much detail as the front, and vents are reduced to a minimum. The figures usually stand on a thin rectangular base. The drapery is generally worn tightly stretched in opposing directions, a scheme which allows for many subtle variations.

Other subjects are Aphrodite, standing and seated; women seated; small girls; small boys, sometimes converted into Eros by the addition of wings; and young men. It is highly probable that the 'Tanagra' style originated in works of sculpture. One Athenian tomb-stone of about 320 B.C. shows this style at an early stage, and there are a number of Roman sculptures, copies of Greek originals, which are nothing but enlarged 'Tanagras', The Romans did not restrict themselves to copying these figures direct; ladies would arrange for a portrait-head of themselves to be placed on a Tanagra body.

The repertoire is limited, and there is a certain sameness in the concentration on tightly draped women, but there is enough variety within the self-imposed limits to make these figures probably the most attractive of all Greek terracottas.

The religious element is less apparent then in previous periods, and it has been suggested that we have here contemporary men and women. This is not always so. Gods and goddesses are humanized in accordance with the spirit of the times, but an attribute here and there reveals who they are. Ivy-leaves in the hair denote a Maenad; a mask held in the hand indicates a Muse; wings on a very human little boy make an Eros (or Cupid); and semi-nudity at this date almost certainly indicates Aphrodite. Colour plate C shows a typical Tanagra lady. She stands on a low plinth, holding up her drapery with her right hand and grasping a fan with her left. In her hair are ivy leaves and berries, and we should therefore regard her not as an ordinary mortal, but as a Maenad, one of the female attendants of Dionysus. Such a ladylike Maenad would be inconceivable at an earlier period, but these Tanagra ladies are somewhat impersonal figures, whose identity can be changed by the manipulation of accessories: a mask would have turned her into a Muse, a mirror into Aphrodite.

She wears the costume of the time, a thin chiton and a tightly draped mantle. The colour is here unusually well preserved, and gives an idea of the original appearance of this piece, with the blue chiton and the pink mantle.

On pl. 12 is another figure of this class. Here the lady is dressed for out-of-doors, in a chiton, a mantle going right over the head and on top a shady hat. The hat is like a Chinese coolie hat, and was fastened to the

C *Tanagra figure, about* 300 B.C.

D   *Women gossiping, from Myrina* (?), *second century* B.C.

mantle with hat-pins. In her right hand she holds a fillet of wool, of the kind used to decorate a statue or a tomb-stone, and we may imagine her to be setting out on such an errand. The degree of tension in the modelling of the body tells us that it belongs to the late Tanagra period, and suggests a date round 250 B.C. This piece has completely lost the frontality of earlier statuettes, and can be seen with enjoyment from almost any point.

On pl. 13 is an unusually elaborate version of a theme, the knuckle-bone player, which originated about 360 B.C. and continued into the Early Hellenistic period. This group, which was made about 320 B.C., was found at Capua in South Italy, and was made there or thereabouts. Two women are squatting on a high rectangular plinth, playing the game of knucklebones. Bones from the ankle-joints of cloven-footed animals, or copies of them in stone or bronze, were used as dice, and were also used (as in this group) for a game played by women and known as 'five-stones', a name current today for the same game.† The object is to throw the bones into the air and catch them on the back of the hand. This group recalls a famous painting of the same subject from Herculaneum.

In the Late Hellenistic period, which covers the second and first centuries B.C. and the first few years of the Christian era, we see a change in Greek terracottas. Gone are the limited repertoire and the elegant poses of the Tanagra style. Some of the subjects may have been observed direct from life, but most are direct copies or adaptations of works of sculpture. Terracottas may now, like contemporary sculpture, be appreciated from any angle.

Although, like the Tanagra style, the Late Hellenistic was a universal one, there is one area in which a higher proportion of first-class work was produced than anywhere else in the Greek world. The cemeteries of Myrina, on the coast of Asia Minor near Smyrna, are to Late Hellenistic figures what those of Tanagra are to Early Hellenistic. The terracotta industry of Tanagra appears to have ceased production about 200 B.C., and from this date the real importance of Myrina is felt. Terracottas start here in the third century B.C. but are not in general as

---

† *Also known as "jacks"*

fine as those of Tanagra at that period.

The cemetery at Myrina was for many years robbed by peasants but was systematically excavated from 1880 to 1882 by French archaeologists. Many terracotta figures were found, the best collections of which are in the National Museum in Athens and in the Louvre, but the British Museum has a few excellent examples, from which those illustrated in pls. 14–16 and colour plate D are taken.

Colour plate D shows two women gossiping on a couch. It was probably made in the second century B.C. To the charm of the Tanagra figures is added a freedom of movement and a choice of subject which denotes a somewhat later period. The one on the right, evidently the elder, bends her head to listen to the other who appears to be telling her a secret. The women's flesh is pink; the couch is red at one end and the hangings are blue. Another second-century piece is illustrated on pl. 14. A naked woman, who must be Aphrodite, leans to her right against a herm of Dionysus, and places a wreath on it. The herm was a square pillar which served as a base for heads of gods. The form, originally restricted to Hermes, was later used for all gods. The exact significance of this theme eludes us, but we can nevertheless appreciate the superb craftsmanship.

Pl. 15 shows a figure of Nike, the goddess of Victory, flying down to earth and holding out in her right hand a wreath with which to crown a victor – whether a victor in a battle or an athletic contest we do not know. The pose is that of the famous Victory from Samothrace in the Louvre. This piece is not very easily dated but it was probably made in the later second or the earlier first century B.C. It is a composite terracotta made up of many pieces. About a dozen separate elements may easily be counted, to include the head, body, limbs, wings and minor attachments.

Pl. 16 shows Aphrodite standing with her arms half-raised; she is evidently putting on a necklace. Her body is elongated and the drapery clings to her body and legs in looped folds. In spite of the unnatural proportions and the equally unnatural treatment of the drapery, this piece has a charm denied to many more lifelike terracottas. This treatment of drapery, which probably originated in the Eastern Mediterranean, was later taken over at Palmyra and even in India.

The date of this Aphrodite is probably the late first century B.C. It is signed on the back with the name of the maker – or perhaps the workshop proprietor – Menophilos. It was the custom at Myrina, and at other centres in Asia Minor, from the late second century B.C. to the early first century A.D. for certain pieces to be signed. These signatures are very useful to students, since pieces bearing the same name were almost certainly made more or less at the same time. The most prolific artisan (or proprietor) at Myrina was Diphilos, but Menophilos did the better work.

Although less complete and less skilfully made, the terracottas from Delos are equally important for this period. Many have been excavated in houses and deposits which date from the early first century B.C. (the island was sacked in 88 and 69 B.C.), and are thus extremely useful for the dating of similar pieces from elsewhere. These terracottas are not represented in the collections of the British Museum, but can be seen in the Museum on Delos.

The production of terracottas did not cease when the Hellenistic period gave way to the Roman Empire. For at least four centuries terracottas continued to be made, especially in the eastern part of the Empire. In some areas, especially in Egypt, standards were still high, but generally speaking there is little to be said for Roman terracottas. One reason for the decline was undoubtedly the increasing cheapness of bronze, which was now within the reach of those who would previously have been content with clay.

The real decline started in the fourth century A.D., when the workmanship became extremely crude. In the fifth century the craft seems virtually to have died out, doubtless because it was too deeply rooted in paganism to survive the triumph of Christianity.

The story of Greek terracottas, in its broadest sense, may be said to cover some 4,000 years of more or less continuous development. In the narrower sense with which this survey has been chiefly concerned, the craft endured in its characteristic form from the seventh to the first century B.C. In this period we have seen how from humble beginnings the Greek terracotta gradually evolved into a real work of art, reaching its culmination in the third and second centuries. B.C., and declining slowly for some centuries thereafter. At its worst the Greek terracotta was the dullest hackwork; at its best, it could take its place amongst the minor arts of antiquity.

Glossary

AEGIS: A special kind of breastplate worn by Athena; it was decorated with a gorgon's head.

CHITON: A linen dress, partially shaped to the figure, and clinging tightly to it.

GLAZE: See p. 11.

MATT PAINT: See p. 11.

PEPLOS: A thick woollen dress, worn draped and falling in heavy folds.

POLOS: A tall cylindrical crown worn by goddesses.

VOTIVE FIGURES: Terracottas when offered to a deity in a temple or a shrine are referred to as votive offerings or votive figures.

Bibliography

GENERAL WORKS
T. B. L. Webster, *Greek Terracottas* (Penguin Books, Harmondsworth, 1950).

SEVENTH CENTURY TERRACOTTAS
R. J. H. Jenkins, *Dedalica* (Cambridge, 1936).

ARCHAIC TERRACOTTAS
P. Knoblauch, *Studien zur archaisch-griechischen Tonbildnerei in Kreta, Rhodos, Athen und Boeotien* (Bleicherode, 1937).

HELLENISTIC TERRACOTTAS
G. Kleiner, *Tanagrafiguren* (Berlin, 1942) .

EXCAVATION REPORTS
Athens. *Hesperia*, volumes I ff.
Corinth. *Corinth*, vols. XII and XV.
Delos. *Délos*, vol. XXIII.
Olynthus. *Olynthus*, vols. IV, VII and XIV.
Rhodes. *Clara Rhodos*, vols. III, IV, VI–VII, VIII.
   Lindos, vol. I.

RECENT MUSEUM CATALOGUES
British Museum. H. B. Walters, *Catalogue of the Terracottas in the British Museum* (1903). R. A. Higgins, *Catalogue of the Terracottas in the British Museum*, vol. I (1954); vol. II (1959).
Danish National Museum, Copenhagen. N. Breitenstein, *Catalogue of Terracottas* (Copenhagen, 1941).
Louvre. S. Mollard-Besques, *Catalogue raisonné des figurines et reliefs*, vol. I (1954)

❧ *List of plates*

Numbers prefaced by the letters B, C, and D refer to the *Catalogue of Terracottas* by H. B. Walters (1903). Numbers not prefaced by a letter refer to the *Catalogue of Terracottas*, vol. I by R. A. Higgins (1954). Numbers in the form 1956, 7-19. 1 are the registration numbers of uncatalogued pieces.

COLOURED PLATES

A   No. 897. Demeter and Persephone. From Thebes (?). Corinthian. About 620 B.C. Ht. 6½ ins. The strut under the seat is modern.

B   No. 970. Aphrodite and Eros. From Olbia, in South Russia. About 350 B.C. Ht. 6½ ins.

C   C 295. Maenad (?). From Tanagra. Boeotian. About 300 B.C. Ht. 9¼ ins.

D   C 529. Women gossiping. From Myrina (?). Second century B.C. Ht. 8 ins.

BLACK AND WHITE PLATES

1*a*   B12. Mycenaean goddess. From Melos (?). 1400–1300 B.C. Ht. 3¼ ins.

 b   B7. Mycenaean goddess. From Athens. 1400–1200 B.C. Ht. 3¾ ins.

 c   B5. Mycenaean goddess. From Athens (?). 1300–1200 B.C. Ht. 4¼ ins.

2   No. 14. Mourning woman. From Camirus. Rhodian. About 670 B.C. Ht. 8¾ ins.

3   No. 779. Goddess. From Tanagra. Boeotian. 575–550 B.C. Ht. 9½ ins.

4   Left: No. 58. Aphrodite. From Camirus. East Greek. About 540 B.C. Ht. 10 ins. Right: No. 57. Aphrodite (scent-bottle). From Camirus. East Greek. About 540 B.C. Ht. 10¼ ins.

5   No. 660. Athena. Unknown provenance. Athenian. About 500 B.C. Ht. 6 ins.

6*a*   No. 806. Man riding a goose. From Tanagra. Boeotian. About 480 B.C. Ht. 4⅝ ins.

30

b No. 958. Monkey. From Tanagra (?). Corinthian. About 420 B.C. Ht. 3½ ins.

7*a* No. 674. Woman standing. From Lake Copais. Athenian. About 450 B.C. Ht. 9 ins.
 b No. 846. Woman standing. From Lake Copais. Boeotian. About 430 B.C. Ht. 15 ins.

8*a* No. 746. Comic actor; young woman. From Athens. Athenian. About 350 B.C. Ht. 5⅝ ins.
 b No. 743. Comic actor; slave on altar. From Peiraeus (?). Athenian. About 350 B.C. Ht. 4¾ ins.
 c No. 973. Doll. From Corinth. Corinthian. About 350 B.C. Ht. 7 ins.

9 1956. 7–19. 1. Goddess. Unknown provenance. Sicilian Greek. About 500 B.C. Ht. 8½ ins.

10 1956. 7–19. 2. Hera. Unknown provenance. Made at Paestum. About 400 B.C. Ht. 8¾ ins.

11 No. 1354 *bis*. Persephone and Iacchus (?). Unknown provenance. Tarentine. About 350 B.C. Ht. 9½ ins.

12 C 312. Woman in outdoor dress. From Tanagra. Boeotian. About 250 B.C. Ht. 7½ ins.

13 D 161. Women playing knucklebones. From Capua. About 300 B.C. Total ht. 5½ ins.

14 C 528. Aphrodite. From Myrina. Second century B.C. Ht. 8⅞ ins.

15 C 533. Victory. From Myrina. First century B.C. Ht. 9¼ ins.

16 1906. 3–10. 1. Aphrodite. Unknown provenance (Myrina type). Late first century B.C. Ht. 10¾ ins.

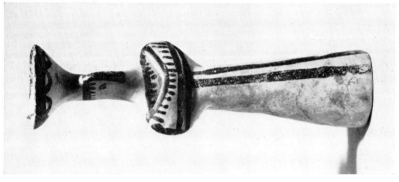

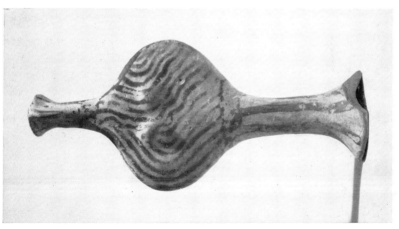

1   *Mycenaean goddesses*, 1400-1200 B.C.

2 *Mourner, about* 670 B.C.

3   *Boeotian goddess*, 575-550 B.C.

4 *Two statuettes of Aphrodite, about* 540 B.C.

5 *Athena, about* 500 B.C.

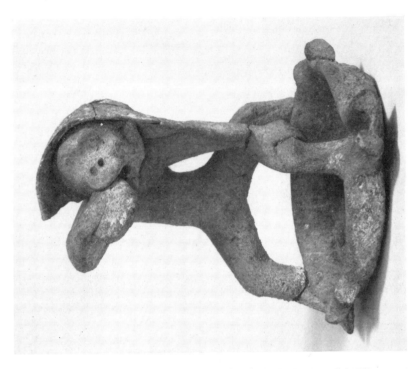

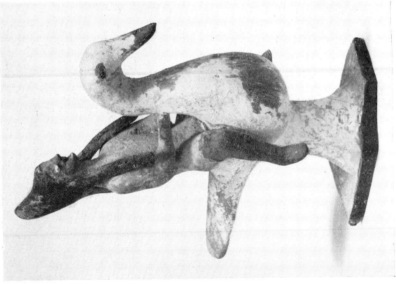

6a *Man on goose, about* 480 B.C.   b *Monkey, about* 420 B.C.

a *Woman, about* 450 B.C.   b *Woman, about* 430 B.C.

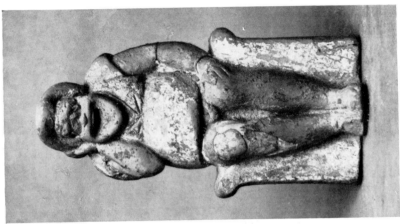

8a & b *Actors, about* 350 B.C.   c *Doll, about* 350 B.C.

9 *Sicilian goddess, about* 600 B.C.

10   *Hera, about* 400 B.C.

11   *Tarentine group, about* 350 B.C.

12 *Tanagra figure, about* 250 B.C.

13 *Knucklebone players, about* 300 B.C.

14   *Aphrodite, from Myrina; second century* B.C.

15   *Victory, from Myrina*; *first century* B.C.

16   *Aphrodite, Myrina type; first century* B.C.